THE CITY OF
BATH

PHOTOGRAPHS BY
COLIN BAXTER

First published in Great Britain in 1990 by
Colin Baxter Photography Ltd.,
Unit 2/3, Block 6,
Caldwellside Industrial Estate,
LANARK, ML11 6SR.

British Library Cataloguing in Publication Data
Baxter, Colin
The City of Bath
1. Avon, Bath
I. Title
942.3980859

ISBN 0-948661-12-7 Hbk
ISBN 0-948661-14-3 Pbk

Front cover photograph
The City of Bath at Dusk

Back cover photograph
The Paragon and Camden Crescent

Text written by Bruce Crofts

Printed in Great Britain by
Frank Peters Printers Ltd., Kendal.

THE CITY OF
BATH

PHOTOGRAPHS BY
COLIN BAXTER

COLIN BAXTER PHOTOGRAPHY, LANARK

INTRODUCTION

No town more honestly reveals its origin by its name than Bath. Even in Roman times it was known as Aquae Sulis, the waters of Sul. During the 18th century the place was widely known as 'The Bath'.

For distant prospect there is much to be said for approaching Bath by the old coaching road from London down Kingsdown Hill, which leads through the village of Bathford. Choose a clear morning, for the evening sun may spoil your view as it did for Jane Austen:

> The appearance from the top of Kingsdown was all vapour, shadow, smoke and confusion . . . I think I see it more distinctly through rain.

BATH IN THE 18th CENTURY

Whereas we make a great song about the character of Bath's wonderful buildings, it is interesting to speculate that most of those who came in this heyday period of Bath were drawn for the comfort they were promised. Thus Philip Thicknesse, author of The New Prose Bath Guide and associate of Thomas Gainsborough:

> It is in Bath alone where People of Fashion can step out of their carriages after a long journey into Houses or Lodgings, full as warm and comfortable as their own . . .
> It is in Bath alone where men of every age can, within a small Compass and at little Expence, find such amusements as are suitable to their inclinations.

There were critics of course and if John Wesley called it 'Satan's Throne', and his brother Charles dubbed it 'That Sodom of our Land', this only confirms that Bath undoubtedly attracted the contemporary hedonistic aristocracy. Saucy behaviour in the baths and formal dalliance on the terraces opened the way to all sorts of romantic relationships. Richard Nash, the Master of Ceremonies and director of the gaming tables set standards of behaviour and earned the title of 'King of Bath'.

PALLADIAN MASTERPIECE

Progress in transforming a medieval township into a Palladian masterpiece was so swift that John Wood, the architect – dreamer, found himself claiming after only 21 years that 'the best chambers for gentlemen were then what the garrets for servants now are'. And by all accounts that was no exaggeration. Stephen Bayley recently put forward the view in the Sunday Times that the Georgians expressed their values '. . . in a style whose graceful strength comes from the variety that can be achieved within strictly defined limits'.
According to David Gadd in Georgian Summer:

> A city which in 1700 was still mediaeval, provincial and insalubrious became in less than a generation the hub of the fashionable world, and within 100 years could be compared with Florence.

There were doctors in abundance to treat the visitors privately with advice about drinking and bathing in the hot spring water. The 100 bed General Hospital, opened in 1742 under Dr. Oliver, and one of the first national hospitals outside London, did much to relieve sufferers of all classes from skin

diseases, lead poisoning and 'rheumatics'. Its long history and current activity are well worth studying.

An air of malaise developed towards the close of the century. Moneyed pleasure seekers and invalids became few. Banks foreclosed on building speculators. Two factors were predominantly responsible for this change in the city's fortunes. First, the Napoleonic Wars absorbed finance and demanded serious attention. Secondly, the strange attraction of sea-water bathing and the pursuit of Royal patronage drew the fashionable visitors to the south coast. Brighton inherited what Bath had initiated.

FASHIONABLE

Bath was fighting for survival as a tourist attraction. Better shops, new pleasure gardens and open air entertainments were widely advertised, but the old days would not return. Moral values were now being emphasized. The fashionable had become the respectable. The playground for the affluent became a paradise for pensioners.

A generation of 'improvers' was now let loose on the city. The Abbey was provided with flying buttresses, stained glass windows and an ornate ceiling over the nave. Street corners were rounded off and carved figures embellished the facades. New shopping parades were developed, railways and improved roads made travel easier while superior hotels provided comfort at the journey's end. The discovery in the 1880's of the Roman Baths and their development on a well designed site served to attract visitors, particularly from abroad.

Sadly against this, the smoke from thousands of grates attacked the limestone of the Woods' and Baldwin's architectural masterpieces and turned them black; virginia creeper became popular though not adding to the damage. More recently acid rain has eaten into the fabric and discoloured those elaborate carvings that expose a large surface area to the elements. It is calculated that a thorough washing down of buildings is needed every 10 to 15 years in cases where heavy traffic is near.

Most of Bath can be seen comfortably on foot. It is hard to believe that 85,000 people live here. Most of the modern housing – of which there is plenty – is tucked away out of sight from the city centre. Views of the city reveal great tongues of country-side invading the built-up areas. The River Avon and its adjacent canal provide pools of cool retreat. Apart from the inevitable industrial sectors there is always rural charm within easy striking distance.

Abandoned by the National Health Service, and then cursed by the appearance of potentially deadly amoebae in the hot springs, the health-giving side of the business closed down in 1977. Bath was a spa no longer. Happily these problems were largely overcome by the driving of a new bore-hole. The legendary benefits of the springs are once more becoming available.

It was the late Sir Kenneth Clark who declared in 1963, when supporting the 'Save and Restore Bath Appeal': 'If there are such things as national treasures, Bath is one of them.' That treasure trove is generously displayed in this book, for all to share.

Bruce Crofts.

THE CIRCUS

John Wood laid the foundation stone of his magnificent King's Circus in 1754 but died three months later. It was originally intended to be part of a grand Roman scheme encompassing this area 'for the exhibition of sports', but in what way is not clear. The circle of houses with three tiers of paired columns, respectively, Roman Doric, Ionic and Corinthian certainly reminds one of the Colosseum turned inwards. Tremendous efforts have been made to restore the stonework to its original honey colour and the continued threat of attack means constant vigilance and regular maintenance. All the Georgian glazing bars have now been restored.

DOORWAY, LANSDOWN ROAD

This is a classical design from the 1770's. Little details reveal their own story. The corrosive effects of coal smoke and traffic fumes are clearly seen on the building, though the stonework facing the prevailing rain remains clear. There were no metalled roads for the first 100 years of the existence of this house. The wrought-iron boot-scraper was a useful precaution against muddy feet.

ABBEY GREEN

This haven of peace was originally within the walled precincts of the monastery. Several of these buildings pre-date Georgian times and were given an 18th century facelift to smarten them up.

THE HIGH STREET

There were once three inns in the High Street dating back to the 1600's: the White Lion, the Greyhound and the Christopher. Sadly only the latter survives and with the new facade illuminated here in oblique light. John Wesley sometimes stayed at the Christopher as the proprietors were Methodists.

The building next to the Abbey stands alongside Wade's Passage. General Wade, who died in 1748, was four times MP for Bath and was responsible for removing the clutter of houses which had forced the public to use the Abbey as a thoroughfare between opposite parts of the city. It is hard to believe that most of the lower parts of the Abbey walls seen here, were once hidden by houses built hard against them.

SKYLINE WITH ABBEY SPIRES

A CORNER OF
ABBEY CHURCH YARD

Al fresco meals were very popular in
Georgian times, particularly breakfasts.
The custom of risking the elements and
enjoying food in the open air is now
returning. This corner of the Church
Yard opposite the Pump Room catches
the sun; the tables are quickly filled in
drier weather.

BATH ABBEY

This church, though young as cathedrals go, stands on one of the most hallowed spots in England. In AD 781, a Saxon church built largely from stones recovered from Roman ruins was dedicated here. In what was then the largest church in the land, on Whit-Sunday in AD 973 the Archbishops of Canterbury and York crowned Edgar the first king of all England. The rituals then followed have been part of the Coronation ceremony ever since.

The Normans came and conquered. In 1107, Bishop John de Villula began to replace the Saxon church by a vast new cathedral 354 feet long and 72 feet wide. Today's Abbey is 202 feet long. The complex when complete included a palace, cloisters, and all the ancillary buildings needed for a self-contained community. They also used the hot springs for their health and comfort.

Henry VII's secretary, Oliver King, was appointed Bishop of Bath and in 1499 by his decree a new cathedral was built in what was just the nave of the then ruined Norman building. As the Norman nave pillar foundations were re-used, the tower had to be rectangular, 32 feet by 20 feet, and the transepts were inevitably narrow.

It was an unpropitious time to build. Although the main framework and tower were completed, including detailed work such as the fan-vaulting and chantry at the eastern end, the decrees of Henry VIII in the 1530's to dissolve the monasteries stopped all work, and led to the plunder and eventual sale of all the property – for £695. However, a visit in 1574 by a disgusted Queen Elizabeth I set building in motion again.

Bath Abbey was the last of the English Perpendicular style

churches to be built. Its condition today is the outcome of steady improvement over 400 years including much work in Victorian times. Particular points of interest are:

The lack of 'dim religious light'. The church is bright, high and happy. Over three-quarters of the wall space consists of windows. Touches of earthy humour may be found by the discerning.

Perfection in masonry is displayed in the fan-vaulted ceilings and perhaps pre-eminently in Prior Birde's chantry which with its delicate tracery is one of the architectural treasures of England. Nearby is the sole surviving Norman arch, though other fragments with even earlier Saxon relics are housed in the Vestry.

The influence of the calendar. There are 4 large pillars, 12 main pillars, 7 doors and 52 windows.

No less than 614 memorial tablets have been placed on the walls, many being specialised works of art. Burials beneath the nave floor are more concentrated than anywhere else in England, such was the clamour to enjoy the Abbey's 'snug-lying'.

Before 1870 there was little seating in the nave; 'the weakest went to the wall' where the stone benches stand.

The West Front displays Oliver King's vision of ladders joining heaven and earth, with angels, some travelling upside-down, symbolising two-way traffic with heaven. Above is the seated figure of Christ in Glory surrounded by the heavenly host. Humans at the lower levels are encouraged by the presence of the 12 apostles. The patron saints, Peter and Paul, guard the door over which stands the statue of King Henry VII.

THE ABBEY, WEST DOOR

The Great West Door in oak was presented in 1618 by Lord Chief Justice Sir
Henry Montagu on the death of his 50 year old brother James, who was Bishop
of Bath and Wells from 1608 to 1616. The left shield shows the Winchester
Diocese Coat of Arms with the Montagu Arms, the whole surrounded by the
insignia of a Knight of the Garter. The right shield repeats the Montagu Arms.
The door was copied and restored in 1833.

THE ABBEY FROM THE SOUTH-EAST

The rectangular tower contains a ring of ten bells. The tenor bell carries the inscription:

All you of Bathe that heare me sound
Thank Lady Hopton's Hundred Pound

However, this suggestion did not receive universal approbation; the pealing caused so much din that the tower had to be shuttered to muffle the sound.

THE PUMP ROOM AND ABBEY CHURCH YARD BY NIGHT

This is the very heart of the city. It teems with life during waking hours. In the past, these buildings have represented two dominating and sometimes opposing influences: religious piety and social pleasure. However, the passing years have seen a gradual softening of attitudes.

THE ABBEY'S EAST WINDOW FROM WITHIN

The great square-headed East Window conforms in its
proportions to Euclid's 'Golden Rectangle' and is a memorial
to the 16th century philanthropist, Thomas Bellott.
It was blown out in the 1942 bombing. By the infinite
patience of the great-grandson of the original designer,
Mr Farrar Bell, it was all restored.
It comprises the largest square-headed church window
in the land (817 square feet of glass) and portrays
56 New Testament stories. The 28 pictures detailed here tell
much of the story of the life of Jesus, particularly the Nativity
and some of the miracles.

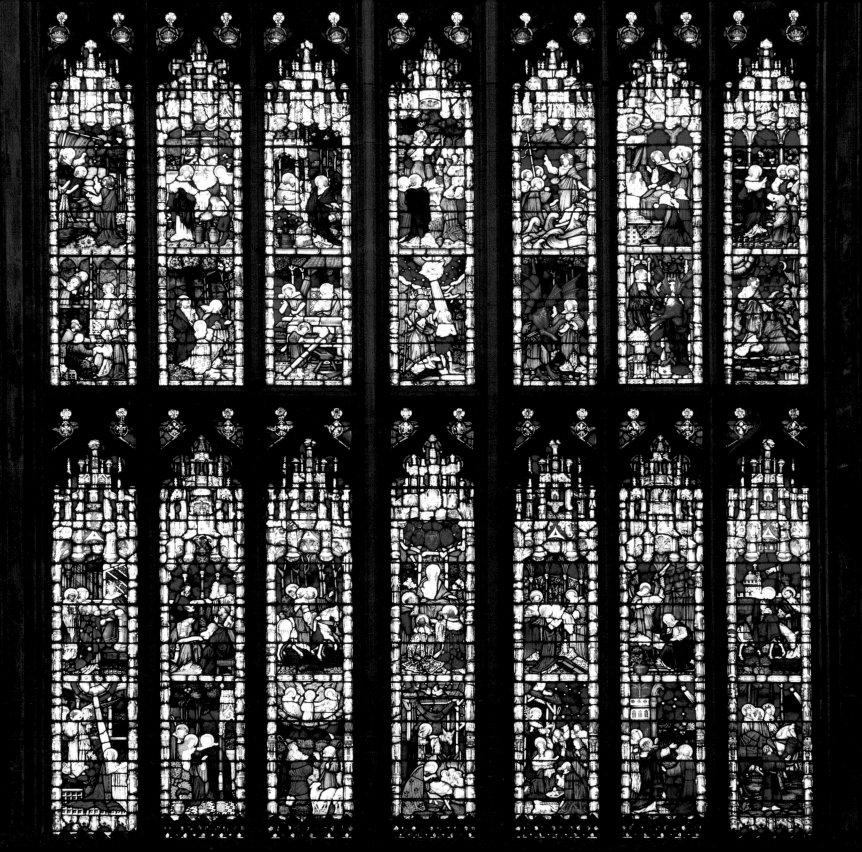

BELMONT, LANSDOWN ROAD

Steep hills require special treatment. Built around 1770, the 20 houses in this terrace include 12 abnormally and individually stepped up so that the remaining eight could be built on the flat. All have staircases leading from the street so that the principal rooms can be at the back to enjoy the view.

FRONT GARDEN BICYCLES

THE PULTENEY BRIDGE

A need arose in the late 1760's to develop land across the river for city expansion. The ferry had to be replaced by a bridge. The Pulteneys, who owned the land involved, arranged for their friend Robert Adam, the most fashionable British architect of the time, to design a unique bridge. Although attempts have been made to compare it with others also having shops along both sides, there is really little resemblance.

The builder took five years to complete the job and went bankrupt in the process. Then some of the shops collapsed into the river and reconstruction was needed in 1804. The southern aspect shown here has been restored. The dominating feature is the central Venetian window with slender Doric half-columns.

There are pavilions at each end of the bridge.

The horse-shoe shaped weir below the bridge replaced the older straight one in 1972 as part of a much needed scheme to protect the city from flooding. It is an aesthetic and engineering success.

ABBEYGATE STREET

Fine floral displays are found even in the back streets of Bath.

HAY HILL

Simple doorways from the late
18th century.

BATH STREET

Bath Street links the Pump Room and its adjoining baths with
the Cross Bath. It was designed by Thomas Baldwin in 1791 to
provide easy access through covered ways beneath the upper
stories which were lined on both sides by Ionic columns.
In 1909 the Grand Pump Room Hotel stood behind
this colonnaded walk which they owned and proposed
to absorb into their hotel.
This would have involved removing these columns. The
scheme caused such an outcry that an 'Old Bath Preservation
Trust' was formed. This eventually succeeded in forcing the
Council to abandon the project.
The building was later converted to become the Spa Treatment
Centre, and more recently a new shopping centre, The
Colonnades, has been created here.

THE PARAGON AND CAMDEN CRESCENT

The Paragon in the foreground faces the wrong way. Its principal rooms are towards the back and look out over the Avon valley. Dating only two years after the Royal Crescent, this shallow terrace by Thomas Atwood was intended to house those of relatively modest means, like Jane Austen's aunt, Mrs Leigh-Perrot.

Camden Crescent came 20 years later. Its architect was John Eveleigh and it was supposed to consist of 22 houses, but when building approached the eastern end, a land-slip prevented the last four houses from being completed. Consequently it stands as a crescent with a centre which is not in the middle. To have five central columns is said by purists to be an architectural solecism.

The dominating chimneys explain why Bath in winter was so often shrouded in smoke. Happily, the introduction of smokeless zones and central heating has cleared the atmosphere.

SALLY LUNN'S HOUSE

The charm of this building lies in its ancient, varied history and the mysterious female cook. Sadly there is virtually no written evidence of Sally Lunn's arrival, but legends die hard and local people firmly believe that she came as a protestant Huguenot refugee and baked her buns here from 1680 onwards. She would have witnessed the start of the transformation of this small town into a fashionable resort. Being already in the business of serving prepared food, she would have had a head-start over rivals in gaining the custom of Beau Nash and his early contemporaries.

A recipe for 'Sally Lunn's' appeared as a poem in 1796, and another poem published 16 years earlier talks of 'spongy rolls or Sally Lun's'. The local newspaper invited all to partake of 'Sally Lund's' in 1778; verses in 1772 name 'Sally Lun's' being eaten in Spring Gardens Pleasure Ground, just across the river. In the new Sydney Gardens of 1796, still open to visitors today:

> Here in the broiling sun we swallow Tea,
> Charmed with the tweedledum and tweedledee.
> Cram down the muffin and the butter'd bun,
> And that eccentric dainty – Sally Lun.

The raconteur, Philip Thicknesse, even half heartedly blamed a combination of drinking Bath waters and eating a hearty breakfast of Sally Luns for the death of his brother, Richard, in 1741.

Sally Lunn's claims to be the oldest inhabited house in Bath.

Unlike many medieval buildings, this one has survived the great replacement programme of the early 18th century, and stands with its distinctive triangular gable ends still intact. Most authorities think the building faced towards the Abbey Church. Built upon a monastic kitchen, the traditional claim on the historic plaque states that this building was first occupied some ten years before Columbus' voyage across the Atlantic – but the exact details are not known. However, there must have been significant developments of some kind around 1482. A tall narrow-framed house was definitely built by a George Parker in 1622. The ovens beneath it would have facilitated the establishment of a bakery. At this time the passageway was known as 'Segar's Alley'. The name 'Lilliput Alley' was later adopted due to the popularity of *Gulliver's Travels.* Today's 'North Parade Passage' was introduced in the 1860's.

We know, for the deeds are on display, that the building passed into new ownership in 1743 and was renovated to satisfy the higher standards then expected. The masonry has endured well, displaying carefully laid, unusually narrow and straight limestone courses. Each floor is supported by enormous oak beams. Within, there are Adams fireplaces, Tudor hearths and Sheraton cupboards. The wealth of finely preserved details within the house has been lovingly nurtured and repays close examination. Supremely, the 'eccentric dainty' is still baked and served on the premises today.

SALLY LUNN'S KITCHEN AND MUSEUM

Formerly part of the 12th century monastery, the hearth and adjoining oven might have stood apart from other buildings where the wood-smoke could easily escape. These baking facilities, later converted to coal-burning, were incorporated when the house above was erected. The raising of the road level subsequently put the kitchen underground.

THE CITY BY DAY

The setting sun highlights man's ingenuity with soft limestone. The tall spire of St Michael's – inspired it is said by Salisbury Cathedral – contrasts with the humbler and earlier St Swithin's to its right. This clearly demonstrates the difference in the importance of church influence between the 18th and 17th centuries.

THE CROSS BATH

It is said that many generations of Bath children were taught to swim here. This photograph, taken before recent developments, reminds us of the friendly social atmosphere which has made this particular spot so popular through the years.

Of the three hot springs in Bath, the one that serves the Cross Bath is the coolest. Bathing could therefore be prolonged. John Leland, who visited in 1542, tells us it was: . . . *much frequented by People diseasid with Lepre, Pokkes, Scabbes, and Great Aches . . .* The best known bather was Queen Mary of Modena, wife of James II, whose visit in 1687 was intended to cure her sterility and provide a male heir to the throne. The efficacy of these waters was proved by the birth of Charles, known to history as the Old Pretender, and father of Bonnie Prince Charlie.

Nearly a thousand years earlier the spring was in use and received its name when a stone cross was erected to commemorate the death of St. Aldhelm in AD 709. The shape of this bath, the construction of its surrounding wall and roofing, have constantly changed over the ages. Current alterations are therefore not unexpected.

NORTHUMBERLAND PLACE

Bath is renowned for its floral displays. Narrow pedestrianised streets of historic charm with shops of character provide the ideal backcloth.

MILES'S BUILDINGS

The sight of this delightful row of modest Georgian town houses is compensation for a long search to discover them. They are found leading from the raised pavement in George Street. Nobody seems to know who designed them, when they were erected, or indeed who Miles was. They are built on one side only of a wide pavement and face towards the revealing backs of Gay Street and the Circus, in a quiet haven close to the city centre.

NUMBER 8 BATH STREET

This tiny Georgian house opposite the Cross Bath was built as
a City museum before 1800 and subsequently became the
residence of successive Bath Superintendents. It displays two
recently restored statues dating from the 14th century.
One may be Bishop Ralph de Salopia, the other John de Walcot,
who along with King Edward III adorned the city's South Gate
before it was demolished in 1755; but some say the statues
came from the old Guildhall.

THE ROYAL CRESCENT

Sadly, John Wood the architect of early 18th century Bath was never strong. When only 50 he died bequeathing his ideas to his eldest son then only 26. Though the general plan was the father's, his son must be given most credit for this grand concept: a semi-ellipse with a 538 feet axis having 114 three quarter Ionic columns each 22 feet high embracing the first and second floors. And all this to create only 30 houses. 'Perhaps the most perfect essay in urban architecture in the western world' as Barry Cunliffe described it. The work took eight years to accomplish, finishing in 1775. As with so many houses supervised in building by the Woods, uniformity applies only to the front exterior; inside and in particular at the back, individuality triumphs.

Before Victoria Park opened in 1830 there were only meadows and a road between the Crescent and the River Avon due south; hence the one-sided wall, technically a 'ha-ha', to keep cattle off the private lawn without spoiling the view from the houses. A satisfying blend of town and country was thus achieved by dint of careful planning.

In recent years there have been helicopter landings and hot-air balloons are the latest and most colourful users of this elegant strip.

THE LAWN AND THE CRESCENT

This sacred grass has seen many changes. At one time it was proposed to instal decorative fountains pumping hot spring water into the air. The scheme was dropped when the cost was revealed. During World War II the 'Dig for Victory' movement resulted in the whole area being converted into vegetable plots.

NUMBER 9, ROYAL CRESCENT

Individual houses of massive proportions attracted only the wealthy, the renowned or the very bold. Number 9 is a typical example. No sooner was it finished in 1768, than in moved the eccentric Philip Thicknesse with his third wife, the talented Ann Ford. He managed to make as many enemies as friends during his literary career.

Later a veteran of Trafalgar, Admiral Sir William Hargood, moved in to spend his retirement years from 1834 to 1839. Lord Bulwer-Lytton, popular author and poet, was here briefly in 1866. Today most of these houses are divided into apartments.

THE PARAGON

The land for this development was leased in 1768 at a rental of four shillings per foot frontage. The building plans by Thomas Atwood were approved by the Mayor, William Chapman, a year later. Originally named Paragon Buildings, this splendid terrace of 21 classic houses was a costly speculation because of the steep slope at the rear, involving the construction of expensive retaining walls and vaults, though none of this is apparent at the front.

STALL STREET

While the City Authorities take great pride in maintaining their architectural heritage they also derive considerable satisfaction in achieving a high standard in the annual country-wide 'Britain in Bloom' contest. This involves not only civic involvement, but also the displays by traders in the shopping streets and by private individuals.

QUEEN SQUARE

Queen Square, completed in 1735, was one of the first elements in John Wood's grand scheme. The north side, of which this is part, demonstrated how a row of seven houses could display sufficient unity as to be mistaken for one grand palace. Fortunately it has survived relatively intact. The railings segregating the central area were reinstated in 1977 to commemorate the Queen's Silver Jubilee and 250th anniversary of the designing of the Square. An inspection of the rear of these premises will reveal a less attractive jumble. The architect in so many cases paid careful attention only to the front and not the rear.

WOOD STREET

A distinctive example of an early
Georgian door to a superior Bath home.

SION HILL

The High Common marks the north-western limit to Bath's seemingly endless
rows of elegant terraces.

THE PUMP ROOM

It became fashionable to drink Spa water late in the 17th century. Harvey's Pump Room, overlooking the King's Bath, was opened in 1706 so that visitors could imbibe in some comfort while listening to 'a small band of musick'. Enlarged in 1751, the building was replaced by today's much grander Pump Room in 1795. This was designed by Thomas Baldwin, the City Architect, who due to bankruptcy, yielded completion to John Palmer. The latter incorporated on the facade the Greek quotation from Pindar, freely translated: 'Water is best', which overlooks the Church Yard.

THE ROMAN BATHS

It is not easy to gain an impression of what the Roman Baths originally looked like when visiting the sites, particularly if time is at a premium. Not only does one need an enormous amount of imagination; the guidance of experts is also essential. The following factors must be taken into account:

Ground level has risen around 6 metres since Roman times.
Due to flooding, several Roman facilities were constructed at successively higher floor levels.
Roofs and columns have collapsed. Very important portions are missing.
The significant discoveries were made as recently as the 1880's by which time large buildings, such as the Abbey, had permanently masked other important Roman sites.
Much that is visible today, eg. underfloor heating, was originally out of sight.
With excavations still proceeding, new facts continue to emerge.

Let us consider why these invaders built such an elaborate complex at this place. By AD 47 the Romans had driven their frontier road, the Fosseway, through this area. It was an important river and road crossing point that needed guarding. The garrison would have discovered some sort of Celtic shrine dedicated to Sulis at the main source, as well as two smaller springs. Very soon the small town, now named Aquae Sulis, boasted a new temple dedicated to Minerva. This was of classical design with Corinthian columns supporting a pediment in which was set the fearsome Gorgon's head, a treasure of the City's Roman museum.

An important task was to master the spring which was producing 250,000 gallons of hot (46.5C) water every day. Excavations in 1978 revealed how the Roman engineers, with considerable skill, had constructed a reservoir around the spring of oak piles and stone blocks held by iron clamps and faced with lead sheets. A large drain leading to the river controlled the head of water and with a sluice enabled the silt to be periodically cleared. These facilities are still in use today. The strong spiritual significance of this spot is emphasized by the many thousands of sacrificial objects recently recovered here.

To balance a temple dedicated to wisdom and healing there was need of facilities for health and restoration. The Great Bath, like all the local bathing facilities, was always roofed. A smaller, cooler, swimming bath to the east led to some artificially heated hypercaust rooms for 'sauna' effect, having under-floor heating. Further developments were thought to stem from an Imperial decree forbidding mixed bathing. Consequently a new suite of baths was constructed at the west end involving a circular, cold plunge bath, further heated rooms and small pools.

Of the other Roman building we know comparatively little. Certainly the city walls are to be seen, and there is some evidence for shrines and baths near the other two springs, as well as luxury housing.

When the Romans left in the 5th century AD, the baths gradually fell into decay, stones were robbed and the spring became clogged. The gradual rise in building levels eventually covered the complex. Their work lay hidden and preserved beneath tons of rubble until the Great Bath's accidental and dramatic discovery only a century ago.

STATUES, ROMAN BATHS

These statues were created as recently as 1894 by George Anderson Lawson of Edinburgh, and represent Roman leaders associated with the government of Britain. They look down over the principal bath. The carved stonework in the background is contemporary with the statues.

THE GREAT ROMAN BATH

The Romans loved bathing and the Great Bath was the focal point for social enjoyment. In cool weather the steam rising from the surface served to emphasize the good fortune of those living where a natural and endless supply of hot water was available.

THE PUMP ROOM INTERIOR

The Serpentine Gallery once housed a lively orchestra, its
shape accommodated the conductor; in recent times a trio
plays here daily, but at ground level. The fountain still serves
hot water from the spring, and good food is served.
Everything is as it was in the late 18th century. The eye,
the ear and indeed the palate are constantly reminded
of the Georgian era.

THE CIRCUS

Five enormous plane trees of 19th century origin stand in the middle of the circle of houses totally dominating them in summer. This particular house, No 17, was rented by Thomas Gainsborough at 200 guineas a year from 1766 to 1774. In the studio at the rear he probably painted *The Blue Boy* and other masterpieces.

TWILIGHT VIEW FROM BEECHEN CLIFF

The Curve of Camden Crescent above Hedgemead Park is complemented by
the sweep of the Paragon below. The city rises to Lansdown, 'the Long Hill', to
the north, and this begins the Cotswold range of hills.

INDEX OF PLACES